To: Nolan
from
Maria

For Alex, in so many ways

Henry Holt and Company, LLC, *Publishers since 1866*
115 West 18th Street, New York, New York 10011
www.henryholt.com

Henry Holt is a registered trademark of Henry Holt and Company, LLC
Copyright © 2002 by Patrick O'Brien. All rights reserved.
Distributed in Canada by H. B. Fenn and Company Ltd.

Library of Congress Cataloging-in-Publication Data
O'Brien, Patrick
Mammoth / Patrick O'Brien

Summary: Describes what is known of this prehistoric ancestor
of the elephant, based on the preserved remains of mammoth bodies.
1. Woolly mammoth—Juvénilé literature. [1. Woolly mammoth.
2. Mammoths. 3. Prehistoric animals.] I. Title.
QE882.P8 O37 2002   569'.67—dc21   2001002668

ISBN 0-8050-6596-2 / First Edition—2002
Printed in the United States of America on acid-free paper. ∞
10 9 8 7 6 5 4 3 2 1

The artist used watercolor and gouache on Italian watercolor
paper to create the illustrations for this book.

PATRICK O'BRIEN
MAMMOTH

HENRY HOLT AND COMPANY / NEW YORK

TWENTY THOUSAND YEARS AGO, SOMEWHERE IN AMERICA

The primitive hunters bring down the huge mammoth. They will have quite a feast that night!

Gigantic vultures swoop down to gobble up anything the hunters don't take. Only the bones are left behind.

Soon a flood buries the bones in mud.

For 20,000 years, more floods leave more mud. The bones are buried deep beneath many layers of earth.

Until . . .

... construction workers building a new shopping mall find something curious in the ground.

They stop working and call the museum.

A scientist rushes right over. "It's a mammoth!" he says. "And a big one too. Those tusks must be 13 feet long!

"And look at that! Stone spear points were buried with the bones. That means the mammoth must have been killed by human hunters."

People have been finding mammoth bones and tusks for hundreds of years. But it was only about 200 years ago that people finally figured out that these giant bones belonged to some kind of ancient elephant-like animal. Before that they could only guess.

In Siberia huge bones were often seen sticking out of the ground, but no one had ever seen a living animal that would fit the bones. People thought the bones must belong to giant rats that lived underground and died if they came up for a look around. The people believed the bizarre beasts used their mighty tusks for tunneling through the earth.

The bones were considered bad luck, so people wouldn't go anywhere near them.

The Siberians called the beast "mammut." This is where we got our word mammoth.

During the Middle Ages people sometimes found huge mysterious bones. The smartest people in Europe examined these strange finds and decided that they knew exactly what the bones were. They were the remains of 20-foot-tall giants!

In 1519 the Spanish explorer Hernán Cortés was in Mexico. An Indian tribe gave him a strange gift—a "giant's thighbone" that had been found in the ground.

In those days people didn't know about evolution. They thought that the kinds of animals they saw around them had been there since the beginning of time. No one knew that long ago there had been other types of animals that were no longer living.

But apparently they did believe in giants.

In 1901 a villager was walking along the Berezovka River in Siberia when he noticed something strange near the shore.

He couldn't resist taking a piece home with him.

When scientists heard about the big tusk he had found, they hurried all the way from Moscow to dig out the creature. It was a mammoth, and it had been preserved in the frozen ground for 30,000 years. But it was not quite complete. Before the scientists could reach it, wolves had chewed away the flesh of the exposed head, leaving just the skull sticking out of the ground. After a month of cold, hard work they finally removed the mammoth from its icy grave. They even found the mammoth's last meal still in its stomach— 33 pounds of grass and leaves!

In 1977, at a gold mine in Siberia, an alert bulldozer driver found the frozen body of a baby mammoth.

The little mammoth died about 40,000 years ago. It was given the name Baby Dima and can be seen at a museum in Russia.

Dima was about six months old when it died—still too young to grow tusks. It was just 3¹/₂ feet tall.

Because of amazing frozen finds like these, scientists know more about mammoths than they do about any other giant prehistoric creatures.

Mammoths were ancient relatives of elephants. Both the mammoth and the elephant first evolved on the fertile plains of Africa more than three million years ago. But mammoths were wanderers, and over time they ventured out of Africa and spread to the far corners of the earth.

When most people think of mammoths, they think of the woolly mammoth. But actually there were several different kinds. Here are some of them:

WOOLLY MAMMOTH

STEPPE MAMMOTH

IMPERIAL MAMMOTH

COLUMBIAN MAMMOTH

The woolly mammoth is the only kind that has been found frozen in the ground, because it was the only one that lived in very cold lands. The mammoths that lived in warmer areas have been reduced to bones, so no one knows if they had long hair like their woolly cousins. But since they lived in warm places, they probably had hair like modern elephants do—that is, not much.

There were even dwarf mammoths. They evolved on various small islands around the world. Maybe this was because there was not a lot of food on these islands, so really big animals couldn't get enough to eat. Only the smallest mammoths could survive.

On the Santa Barbara Islands off the coast of California there were mammoths that were only 5½ feet tall.

If you went to the island of Malta in the Mediterranean Sea 10,000 years ago, you would see mammoths walking around that were about the size of big dogs.

These tiny giants were only about 3½ feet tall!

This is a chart of the mammoth family tree. All these animals are now extinct except for the last ones, the African and Asian elephants.

The earliest known ancestor of mammoths was Moeritherium. It was about the size of a pig, and had an elongated nose that you might say was almost a trunk.

MASTODON

25 million to 10,000 years ago

The Mastodon was an ancient species that was around long enough to share the North American plains with mammoths.

MOERITHERIUM

45 to 30 million years ago

PALEOMASTODON

36 to 25 million years ago

DINOTHERIUM

25 to 2 million years ago

Dinotherium's tusks were in its lower jaw instead of in its upper jaw, like the tusks of mammoths and elephants.

PLATYBELODON

25 to 7 million years ago

Scientists sometimes call Platybelodon a "shovel tusker."

ANANCUS

6 to 1 million years ago

Scientists aren't sure why Anancus needed such long tusks.

MAMMOTH

3 million to 4,000 years ago

ASIAN ELEPHANT

3 million years ago to today

Asian elephants are more closely related to mammoths than African elephants are.

GOMPHOTHERIUM

18 to 5 million years ago

AFRICAN ELEPHANT

1.5 million years ago to today

Mammoths were closely related to modern elephants, but they were a little different.

MAMMOTH
9–16 feet high
Head had a high single dome on top.

AFRICAN ELEPHANT
10–13 feet high
Head is low and rounded.

ASIAN ELEPHANT
10 feet high
Head has two domes.

Mammoth tusks were much bigger and more curved than elephant tusks.

Elephant ears are bigger than woolly mammoth ears.

A mammoth's back was sloped.

An African elephant's back is saddle-shaped.

An Asian elephant's back is slightly humped.

The tip of a mammoth's trunk had a different shape than the tip of an elephant's trunk.

MAMMOTH
one small "finger" and one wide "finger"

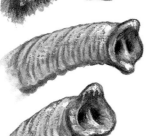

AFRICAN ELEPHANT
two "fingers"

ASIAN ELEPHANT
one "finger"

A mammoth used its trunk to pick grass and to stuff it into its mouth. It probably ate 300 to 500 pounds of grass every day.

It also drank with its trunk by squirting water into its mouth.

And of course a mammoth could smell with it—after all, a trunk is really a long nose.

Woolly mammoths lived in a cold world. There have been many times in the history of the earth when the weather was a lot colder than it is today, and most of the northern parts of the world were covered by ice. These cold periods are called ice ages.

Woolly mammoths lived during the most recent ice age. It began about 1½ million years ago and ended about 10,000 years ago. When people talk about the Ice Age, they usually mean this most recent one.

20,000 YEARS AGO

In some places, the ice was more than two miles thick.

TODAY

There were a lot of really big animals back in the Ice Age.

There were giant armadillo-like creatures called glyptodonts that were ten feet long.

Aurochs were really big cattle that wandered the forests of northern Europe. They were about six feet tall.

The woolly rhinoceros had a front horn that was more than three feet long.

Giant ground sloths in South America were as big as mammoths.

Cave lions and cave bears sometimes chased cavemen out of their homes. These animals were a little bigger than the biggest lions and bears today.

Megaloceros was much bigger than today's deer.

And down in Australia even the kangaroos were bigger. They were about eight feet tall.

Mammoths were so big that most animals couldn't harm them. But there was one kind of animal that they feared: humans. These little two-legged hunters were smaller than mammoths, but they were a lot smarter.

It was easiest—and safest—to go after a mammoth that was very old or very young.

One good kill and they could eat mammoth meat for weeks.

It wasn't easy to bring down such a huge animal, even with the stone spear points they had.

Hunters made the points by using a hard rock to chip away at a more brittle one.

The stone blade was as sharp as a knife.

Sometimes they used traps to catch mammoths.

First they dug a deep hole, then they covered it with branches and leaves to hide it from passing mammoths.

There were so many mammoths in those days that people sometimes made their huts out of the bones. Some huts were made of bones from more than 90 different mammoths!

They started with the tusks and skulls.

Then they used other bones to fill in the gaps.

They covered the hut with mammoth skins, and it was done.

Ice Age people sometimes made paintings deep
inside caves of mammoths and other animals.

*Perhaps they thought that capturing the image of a mammoth on
a cave wall would help them to catch and kill the real thing.*

Mammoths had to watch out for the brave little humans with the long sharp spears. But in what is now Los Angeles, California, mammoths had other things to worry about.

At the place now known as Rancho La Brea in Los Angeles, sticky black tar seeped out of the earth and onto the ground. When animals walked through the tar, their feet got trapped in the oily ooze. Their struggles attracted predators looking for an easy meal. Then the predators got stuck, and soon all the animals died together in the tar.

Sometimes the tar was hidden under a thin layer of water.

Tar rises from deep in the earth.

Scientists began digging into this fossil treasure trove in 1901. Since then they have dug the bones of 34 mammoths from the tar. But most of the animals that died in the tar were predators who had come to feast on trapped animals. The tar-soaked bones of more than 2,000 saber-toothed cats and 3,000 prehistoric wolves have been found in the oily pits.

Here are some of the Ice Age animals that have been found in the tar at La Brea:

Smilodon, the saber-toothed cat

The short-faced bear

The La Brea condor

The mastodon, a relative of mammoths

The long-horned bison

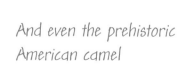

And even the prehistoric American camel

Most mammoths died out about 10,000 years ago, along with most of the other large Ice Age mammals. No one really knows why, but scientists have some ideas.

The world was getting warmer at that time, and the great ice caps were melting away. The changing climate caused major changes in the environment. Some grasslands became forests. Some forests became deserts. The plant life that animals depended on for food began to grow in different parts of the world. Maybe the really big mammals, like mammoths, just couldn't adjust to the new environment.

Some scientists think that it was not the new weather that killed the mammoths but the new humans. In the last part of the Ice Age, about 30,000 to 10,000 years ago, human populations were increasing and spreading around the globe. These scientists say that human hunters wiped out the mammoths by killing too many of them. But other scientists doubt that there were enough humans around at that time to kill off so many mammoths.

Perhaps the mammoths were already dying out because of the changing environment, and the humans just finished them all off—that is, almost all of them.

On a cold, remote island north of Siberia, a small population of mammoths survived up until about 4,000 years ago. These were dwarf mammoths, only about six feet tall, but they managed to scratch out a living for more than 6,000 years after mammoths had died out everywhere else.

So while human civilizations were beginning, and the pyramids were being built along the Nile, far away in the frozen north great shaggy beasts still roamed an icy landscape. They were survivors from an earlier age. They were the last mammoths.

PRONUNCIATION GUIDE

Anancus — ah-NAN-kus

Aurochs — OR-uks

Dinotherium — dine-o-THER-ee-um

Glyptodont — GLIP-toe-dont

Gomphotherium — gom-foh-THER-ee-um

Mastodon — MAS-toe-don

Megaloceros — meg-a-loh-SER-us

Moeritherium — mo-ri-THER-ee-um

Paleomastodon — pay-lee-o-MAS-toe-don

Platybelodon — pla-tee-BEL-o-don

Smilodon — SMILE-o-don